Nature's Wild®

WOLVES

by
Jane P. Resnick

Scientific Consultant:
Edward M. Spevak
Assistant Curator of Mammals
Wildlife Conservation Society/Bronx Zoo

Manufactured in China

0406-1C

Visit us at www.readingchallenge.com

Contents

WOLF!

Dangerous. If we know very little about wolves, this word seems to fit. But wolves are not dangerous to people. They are wild and fierce, like any other animal that hunts to feed itself. And, like all animals, they have their own way of life—separate from humans.

DOG YEARS

The wolf, as it is now, roamed Earth around one million years ago. Wolves *evolved*, or formed, from carnivores (meat-eaters) around 60 million years ago. The *canids* (which include wolves, dogs, and their relatives) separated from the *felids* (cats and their relatives) around 20 million years ago.

COLORFUL COAT ▶

Although known as the gray wolf, its coat is anything but plain gray. The variety of coat colors ranges from pure black to white, with shades of red, yellow, tan, silver, and brown in between. Any of these colors can occur within the very same family.

CANIS TIMES THREE

Scientists believed that there were two types of wolf—the gray wolf, *Canis lupis*, and the red wolf, *Canis rufus*. But recently, scientists have discovered a third type called the Ethiopian wolf, *Canis simensis*. The gray wolf lives in the northern hemisphere, and the red wolf lives only in the southeastern United States. The Ethiopian wolf is found only in Africa.

Red wolf ▲

◄ Gray wolves that live in the high arctic are called arctic wolves.

BIG?

"Big" is not exactly the right word for wolves. They vary in size. The average male weighs 95 pounds and the female, 10 pounds less. They stand $2\frac{1}{2}$ feet high and measure 5 to $6\frac{1}{2}$ feet from the tip of the nose to the end of the tail.

HELPFUL HUNTERS

Wolves live in the mountains, forests, and plains of the northern hemisphere. They have a special role in relation to their environment. It's called their *ecological niche* (pronounced NICH). Wolves are the most numerous of all predators that hunt large mammals in this territory.

REAL CHARACTERS

Like dogs, wolves are very intelligent animals and are capable of learning. Also, each one seems to have its own personality. Some are shy, while others are bold and outgoing. Some are very social within their group, while others hang back.

MEMBERS OF THE PACK

Wolves have a strong social nature. They live as a family, in what is called a *pack*. There is a pecking order within the pack, in which each wolf has a rank. Some wolves are *dominant*—aggressive and forceful. Others are *submissive*, giving in to authority.

A wolf family—called a pack.

BLOOD TIES

A male and female head the wolf pack. They are the core of a group that is related by blood and affection. Other members are their offspring, ranging in age from pups to two or three years old. Most packs have six or seven members, although some may include as many as 15 wolves.

NUMERO UNO

The most powerful male wolf in a pack is known as the alpha (Alpha is the first letter in the Greek alphabet). His mate, the alpha female, helps rule the pack. They have forceful personalities, necessary for their dominant role. They make the decisions that affect the pack's survival.

FANG FIGHTS

Wolves within a pack rarely fight, because the alphas maintain order. However, wolves do fight members of other packs or intruding lone wolves. All wolf packs have a territory of their own. They patrol it and mark it, so that other wolves will know to stay out. If a strange wolf intrudes, it will be attacked and killed.

THE LONE WOLF

Do you know a "lone wolf," someone who stays apart? The expression comes from wolves who go off on their own. A pack grows and changes. Some young adults wait to move up to alpha positions when leaders become old or weak. Other wolves leave to wander and hunt alone, but they may start their own pack if they can find a lone mate.

OMEGA

In larger packs, there are wolves known as omegas (Omega is the last letter in the Greek alphabet). These wolves are picked on by all members of the pack. Sometimes they are bothered so much that they leave the pack.

An angry alpha tells an unwelcome intruder, "Get off my turf!"

9

PACK CONTROL

If two wolves are going to rule a pack, they have to be able to show their authority and keep the others in line. To do so, they constantly dominate the lower-ranking wolves from the moment these wolves are born. The alpha male dominates the other males, and the alpha female keeps the other females in line.

▲(1)The alpha wolf growls at a lower-ranking wolf, who lowers his head.

KIN PIN
Lower-ranking wolves (subordinates) are constantly disciplined by alphas. Alphas growl, bite, chase, and even pin them to the ground while the rest of the pack looks on (1-4).

(2)The alpha bites and tackles ▲ the subordinate.

(3)The alpha pins the ▶ subordinate.

TOP TAIL
A wolf's tail is like a flag waving its rank. Alphas hold theirs high. Wolves below the alphas keep their tails low. And lowest-ranking members tuck their tails between their legs.

▲ This male alpha wolf is holding his tail high.

▲ With her tail tucked between her legs, this subordinate female slinks off.

STERN STARE

A stern, unwavering stare from an alpha wolf is enough to convince members of the pack to bend to his or her authority. Submissive wolves will pull their lips back in a defensive grin, lower themselves to the ground, and, if they can, turn and slink away. Sometimes they roll on their backs to make things very clear that they know who's boss.

YOU'RE THE BOSS

Lower-ranking members show respect and affection for the alpha wolf in a special greeting ceremony. They approach him or her with their bodies low, fur and ears flattened. Then, reaching up, they lick and nip the alpha's face affectionately.

(4)Finally, the lower-ranking wolf begs forgiveness. ▼

11

WOLF TALK

Wolves are among the most loyal of animals, having deep attachments to their companions. Through gestures and body movements, wolves communicate their feelings. This "wolf talk" keeps the pack together and working as a group.

Affection between wolves is shown by nuzzling, licking, and cuddling.

BEGGING FOR BITES

The alpha wolves are usually at the head of the pack when attacking prey. They are the first ones to take bites out of the kill and get the choicest parts to eat. Lower-ranking wolves have to beg for food. They lay their ears back and, with their mouth closed, whine and paw at the alpha's face. Every now and then, they manage to grab some food.

PALS THAT HOWL

To people, the howl of the wolf is the sound of the wild. To wolves, it may be a party. Wolves most often howl as a pack—to encourage their closeness, to celebrate a successful hunt, to find separated members, and to tell other packs to keep back. On a calm night, howling can broadcast 120 square miles.

Alpha wolves make it clear to others that they should wait their turn to eat.

TELLTALE TAIL

A wolf also uses its tail to express how it's feeling. A tail raised and slightly curving up at the tip means the wolf is sure of itself. If the tail is dropped but curved up at the end, the wolf is being friendly. If the tail is between the wolf's legs, the wolf is being friendly or is afraid.

FACE TO FACE

Wolves have very expressive faces. A fearful wolf flattens its ears and covers its teeth in a meek smile. An angry wolf bares its teeth and points its ears forward. A wolf that is threatened and afraid keeps its ears back but also bares its teeth, letting its tongue roll out. These are clear messages, and pack mates know how to react to keep the peace.

This wolf is being threatened and is afraid.

One wolf sits down to show the other that he doesn't want to fight.

13

BUILT FOR HUNTING

At this very moment wolves are hunting. They are physically built to do so. If there is snow, they are leaving a neat line of single tracks, hind feet following exactly behind front feet. This gait occurs because a wolf's legs are spaced very close together. It is an advantage in deep snow and difficult country.

TEETH FOR TOOLS

Teeth are weapons, and wolves have an arsenal of forty-two. Four pointed canines curve out near the front of the jaw, two on top and two on bottom. With these two-inch spikes, a wolf can pierce through tough hides and thick hair and hang on. With their *carnassials*, or molars, adult wolves can crush the thigh bone of a moose.

ON THEIR TOES

When wolves hunt, they are swift and silent—because they run on their toes. Like horses and cats, wolves keep the back parts of their feet raised when walking or running. Moving in such a way, with strong, muscular legs, wolves have long strides. They can trot for long periods at five miles an hour and race up to 40 miles an hour.

RADAR EARS

Hearing is a hunting skill, and wolves have the best. Wolves listen by turning their ears from side to side. By recognizing where the sound is loudest, they can tell the direction the noise is coming from. Ears up, they can hear sounds several miles away.

WOLF PARKA

In order to hunt in winter, wolves are protected by a fur coat as thick as three inches. Nearest to the wolf's flesh is a dense woolly undercoat to keep it warm. Black-tipped guard hairs form a longer, rougher outercoat that shuts out moisture and sheds water. In this fur-lined raincoat, a wolf can go anywhere.

THE NOSE KNOWS

Noses to the air, wolves pick up the scent of prey before they detect it in any other way. If the wind is blowing from the direction of the hunted animal, they can catch the odor as much as a mile and a half away—before they hear or see their prey. Noses down, wolves can also follow fresh tracks with their sharp sense of smell.

This wolf knows how to follow its nose.

15

PACK HUNTERS

Wolves are carnivores (meat-eaters). They are predators that hunt in groups. Sometimes a small animal like a beaver, rabbit, mouse, or bird is a mouthful for a single, hungry wolf. But in order to feed its many members, a pack must kill large prey, such as deer, caribou, elk, moose, or mountain sheep.

DELICATE BALANCE

Wolves are part of nature's scheme. Generally, they kill the old, sick, and young of their prey. Often, the group on which they prey benefits as well. If the sick die, there is less chance of disease spreading. If older animals are killed, there is more food for the young. This "balance of nature" helps keep predator and prey healthy.

GETAWAY PREY

Fierce as wolves may seem, most of their prey escapes. Less than 10% of wolf hunting is successful. In one three-day study, wolves pursued 131 moose but killed only six. What happens? Deer and caribou can outrun wolves. Moose may fight back. That's 1200 pounds of animal with sharp antlers and heavy hooves—enough to crush a wolf's skull.

Usually, bison will defend themselves by grouping and greeting wolves head-on, with weight and horns. Wolves then try to separate one from the herd.

CLEAN PLATE

Food is life, but food is scarce for many wolves. Wolves can survive for two weeks without eating—and gorge themselves when they do. (An adult wolf can eat as much as 20 pounds at one time). Bolting down the flesh of its kill in large pieces, a pack of wolves leaves nothing behind—only the hooves and largest bones.

◀ A wolf is marking its territory.

WE ARE HERE. DON'T INTERFERE.

Survival depends on hunting grounds, and wolves will fight to defend them. A pack's territory ranges from 30 square miles to 800 square miles, depending on the kind of animal they hunt. Borders are posted with scent markings—urine sprayed on tree stumps and rocks—and advertised with group howling.

BURIED TREASURE ▲

Sometimes wolves will store some of their kill by dropping it in a hole and covering it over. Later, when hunting is difficult, they go back to this cache (sounds like "cash") and dig up their buried treasure.

17

PUPPY LOVE

For a wolf pack, new life begins in the spring, when pups are born. Usually, it is the alpha female that has the pups. She is pregnant for nine weeks and takes care of the pups for the first month. After that, the whole pack joins in the responsibility, helping feed them and watch out for them.

◀ A two-month-old wolf, now a member of the pack.

▼ A mother nurses her pups until they are old enough to eat meat

LITTLE LITTER

Blind, deaf, and weighing only one pound—that's a wolf puppy at birth. But the litter of five or six pups grows quickly. At two weeks their eyes open. At three weeks, they weigh as much as seven pounds each and walk on all four legs. At about one month, the pups step out into the world.

DUG OUT

Wolf puppies are born underground in a den. Not just a hole in the ground, a den is a well-planned burrow that is dug by the mother. There's an entrance, just big enough for an adult wolf, and a tunnel at least ten feet long. At the end is a chamber where the pups are born.

▲ A mother watches out for her two nine-week-old pups outside the den.

With a wolf pup and its mother, affection begins early on.

STOMACH STORAGE

To keep her newborn pups warm, the mother wolf has to remain in the den for three weeks after giving birth. Once the pups can eat meat, she and other pack members bring it back to them—carrying it up to 20 miles in their stomachs. The adults then have to "bring up" the food so the pups can eat it!

♥ ♥ ♥ ♥ ♥ ♥ ♥ ♥ ♥ ♥ ♥ ♥

PUP-SITTERS

Once the pups leave the den, the whole pack becomes their protectors. The adult and juvenile wolves watch for predators—like eagles—and keep the pups from wandering off. This caretaking helps bond the newest members to the rest of the pack.

These wolf pups are playing tug-of-war, which will strengthen their bite.

BUSY BODIES

Running, chasing, pouncing, fighting, chewing—all this playing is serious fun for pups. It's how pups strengthen their muscles and develop hunting skills. In playing, they show their personalities, too. One "top dog" pup will want to boss his brothers and sisters around.

AT REST AND AT PLAY

Wolves have to pause to use their paws for scratching.

Wolves don't hunt and growl and look fierce all the time. In fact, after they've eaten, the first thing they like to do is curl up and take a long nap. When they awaken, with a full belly and lots of energy, they like to have fun. Wolves that want to play offer an invitation. They approach other pack mates, bowing low with their front legs on the ground. Their tail wags and says "please." No response? They jump from side to side doing a zigzag dance to get attention, just like a dog.

Wolves love to play in the water.

Wolves can even sleep during a snowstorm.

Water is fun to explore.

Jumping a creek is a sporting test of strength.

This playful young female wolf is showing her brother how to roll around in the snow.

After a meal, the pack is ready for a nap.

21

WOLVES AND PEOPLE

Who's afraid of the big, bad wolf? Most of us. Think of the wolves in the stories *Little Red Riding Hood* and *The Three Little Pigs.* For centuries, folktales have presented wolves as evil. In truth, wolves don't harm people. People kill wolves. And wolves are a threat only to people's livestock—their sheep, cattle, and chickens.

A SAD HISTORY

In the United States, a campaign to kill wolves was launched after Europeans began settling the land. In the 1800 s, people moving into the Great Plains hunted buffalo, which the wolves had always depended on for food. The wolves, therefore, turned to cattle and sheep. To protect their livestock, ranchers started killing the wolves. Perhaps one to two million were killed. Today, there are probably fewer than 10,000 wolves in the United States, and most of them are in Alaska. Canada has as many as 50,000.

Mexican wolves, now endangered, once roamed Arizona, New Mexico, and Mexico.

WOLF RALLY

At one time, wolves lived throughout North America, Europe, and Asia. Outside of Alaska and Minnesota, they have been nearly eliminated from the United States. However, in 1973, the U.S. government passed the Endangered Species Act to protect those animals disappearing from the Earth. In addition, the government has appointed special wolf recovery teams for the Mexican, northern Rocky Mountain, eastern timber, and red wolves.

RANCHERS ROAR

The goal of wildlife biologists is to return wolves to their natural habitats—to places such as Yellowstone National Park. But ranchers and farmers who live near these areas protest because they fear for their livestock.

These wolves have brought down a moose.

WOLF vs. HUNTER

People who hunt big game, like elk and moose, usually go to a specific area, where they use lodges, restaurants, and guides. The people living in this area depend on the business provided by hunters. And they believe that wolves interfere with their livelihood by killing elk, moose, and other big game.

RESCUING RED

Once common in the southeastern United States, the red wolf is nearly extinct—gone forever. Many of the ones that have survived have mated with coyotes. In 1975, in an effort to save red wolves, 400 were captured to be bred and reintroduced into the Southeast. Only 14 of those caught were pure red wolves.

ON THE RADIO

These days, wolves need people to care about them. Conservationists work to save animals and their environment. Wildlife biologists study animals. Wolf collars with radio transmitters help keep track of wolves so that scientists can help the wolves and learn more about them.

A scientist visits a pack living in a wolf park.

European wolf

Red wolf

COYOTE COUNTRY

Although they live only in North America, coyotes are found from Alaska to Costa Rica, throughout Canada, and from the Pacific coast to the Atlantic. They live in Death Valley, California, where the temperature soars to 135°F, and on the plains of Canada, where it drops to -65°F. Today, there are more coyotes than ever before.

IN GOOD VOICE

Coyotes are musical. Their voices have a high and low range. Their howling is very close to singing, with a variety of sounds— barks, huffs, yelps, woofs, and yaps. They recognize each other's voices. When one coyote begins howling, others within hearing distance join in. Mated coyotes keep in touch through howling when separated. They even have a greeting song.

UP TO SIZE

The average coyote is two feet high, four feet long (including its tail), and looks like a medium-sized dog, similar to a German shepherd. Twenty-five pounds is the average weight, although some are as heavy as 70 pounds. Whatever the size, thick fur makes coyotes look larger than they are.

COYOTE COUPLES

Coyotes are social animals that live in family groups. A male and female mate for life or, at least, may stay together for several years. They become much closer in the month before breeding. They hunt together, sing howling duets, and show affection by pawing and nuzzling.

Playing is a way of showing affection.

THE LONE COYOTE

Born in the spring, most coyote pups leave their parents by the fall. They go off to find their own hunting territories. If their parents' area has limited food sources and a large coyote population, they may have to go as far as 100 miles away. They may find mates, raise families, and live six to eight years.

Coyotes are less than one year old when they leave their parents.

These pups are taking a peek at the world from the door of their den.

NIGHT MOVES

Coyotes are excellent parents, guarding their pups carefully. If they suspect that their den is threatened, coyotes will move the pups to another place. Normally, this is nearby. But one female was observed carrying her four pups, one at a time, to a new den five miles away. That's a 40-mile journey in one night.

25

Trotting is a coyote's favorite way to travel.

A coyote blends in with the scenery—until it jumps out and flashes its teeth. ▼

ON THE MOVE

Coyotes are natural wanderers, often traveling up to 50 miles in a single night. If they trot, they can average 20 miles per hour (mph). When they gallop, they can reach 30 mph. Sometimes they run 40 mph—in short spurts. That's fast enough to catch a jackrabbit.

◀ Coyotes can leap up to 14 feet.

CAMOUFLAGE COAT

Coyotes have coats that keep them undercover, so they can sneak up on prey and hide from predators. The ones that live in wooded regions have dark fur, which makes them difficult to see in the underbrush. Desert-dwelling coyotes have tawny coats that blend in with sand and weathered rock.

BUILT JUST RIGHT

Coyotes have the tools to be excellent hunters. With their powerful legs, they can leap up to 14 feet. With keen eyesight, they can see the slightest movement yards away. With their sharp hearing, they can detect the faintest stirrings of mice under the snow. And with a strong sense of smell, they can pick up a human scent and run away to safety.

FULL MENU

Coyotes are not fussy about their food. Scavengers, they will steal a meal stored by other predators. They eat deer, rabbits and other rodents, insects, and fish. They will even plunge into the water after frogs, crayfish, and turtles. Although they are meat-eaters, they will also eat fruits and berries, and they have a special fondness for watermelon.

▲ This coyote is making a meal out of some berries.

◄ A coyote raiding a chicken coop.

SUCCESSFUL SURVIVORS

According to one Native American legend, coyotes will be the last living animal on Earth. In some ways, this is hard to imagine. Ever since the West was settled by non-Indians, people and coyotes have been in conflict. Coyotes eat livestock, such as cattle, sheep, and chickens. Shot, trapped, and poisoned by angry farmers, millions of coyotes have died. Somehow, though, they have "learned" to avoid human hunters.

A coyote caught in a trap.

Coyotes have the ears and nose for detecting even the smallest creatures. ▼

THE WILY COYOTE

Coyotes are clever hunters who some-times hunt in pairs. One of their favorite prey is the jackrabbit, which tends to run in circles. One coyote will chase the rabbit while the other waits at the head of the circle. It's not likely that the rabbit will live to make too many circles.

27

FRIENDS AND RELATIONS

Wolves and coyotes are only two members of the dog family. Domestic and wild dogs, foxes, and jackals are some others. Even though they may look a little different on the outside, they have the same basic structure underneath. Called *canids*, they are all carnivores, with teeth designed for eating meat—long, pointed canine teeth (fangs) at the front, and sharp, shearing molars at the back.

Even the smallest dogs, like this Bichon Frise, are related to wolves.

JACKALS FOR KIN ▶

At a gathering of canids, jackals would have to be invited—all three species—the golden, side-striped, and black-backed. Africa is their homeland, but the golden also lives in Asia and Europe. Although known as scavengers, jackals are excellent hunters. They also have a social nature like that of wolves—they live in a family.

WILD DOG ▲

There's a wild member of the dog family almost everywhere in the world. African wild dogs live and hunt in packs of more than 30 members. They stalk their prey with ears back and head lowered, then chase it in tag teams. They run for several miles at 30 miles per hour, until the prey is brought down.

◀ WILD DINGO!

The dingo is the wild dog of Australia. Dingoes were originally domesticated dogs brought to the island thousands of years ago by the ancestors of natives, the aborigines. Finding themselves in a land with almost no meat-eating predators, dingoes quickly spread across the continent—and went wild.

FOX IN THE FAMILY

The fox is a relative of the wolf, but without its long, full fur, the fox looks more like a stream-lined greyhound. There are 21 kinds of foxes. Although hunted and trapped for their fur, they still thrive throughout the world.

Arctic fox

Red fox

MANED WOLF ▶

The maned wolf looks like a cross between a wolf and a fox. But it is not really a wolf or a fox, although it is named the maned wolf and is some-times called the "stilt-legged fox." A member of the dog family, the maned wolf lives in southern Brazil and hunts by pouncing on small animals.

HUSKY COUSIN ▼

The Siberian husky is a breed of working dog that originated in northeastern Siberia many centuries ago. In the early 20th century, it was brought to Alaska, where it is still used as a sled dog, particularly in the sport of sled team racing. Because it's intelligent and friendly, the husky also makes a great pet.

The husky is a wolflike dog that is used in the far North to pull sleds.

Glossary

Alpha wolves: The alpha wolves are the dominant male and female of the wolf pack. (*Alpha* is the first letter of the Greek alphabet.)

Canidae: The scientific classification for the dog family, which includes wolves, coyotes, wild and domestic dogs, foxes, and jackals.

Canis lupis: Scientific name for a gray wolf.

Canis rufus: Scientific name for a red wolf.

Carnassials: Large molars in the back of a carnivore's mouth that are especially suited for cutting rather than tearing flesh.

Carnivore: An animal that eats the flesh of other animals.

Communicate: To exchange information. Wolves communicate through sound and movement.

Conservationist: A person who works to keep Earth's resources safe, and to protect animals and their habitats.

Den: The place where an animal, such as a wolf or bear, sleeps. Wolf dens are underground burrows.

Dominant male: The most important male in a flock, clan, or gathering of animals. The dominant male wolf makes decisions for the rest of his pack.

Ecological niche: The special role an animal plays in its environment.

Endangered: Threatened with extinction. Certain species of animals are in danger of becoming extinct (dying out).

Endangered Species Act: An act of Congress that requires the U.S. government to protect animals and plants threatened with extinction, as well as their habitats.

Evolve: To gradually change or develop.

Extinction: The death of a population of animals caused by loss of habitat, predators, or the inability to adapt to changes in the environment.

Habitat: The place where an animal or plant naturally lives and grows.

Litter: The offspring of an animal, such as a wolf.

Lone wolf: A wolf that is not part of a pack. A lone wolf will sometimes start its own pack if it can find a lone mate.

Omega wolves: Wolves with the lowest status in the pack; they are picked on by all its members. (*Omega* is the last letter in the Greek alphabet.)

Pack: Gathering or clan of wolves. Wolf packs usually have six to fifteen members.

Predator: An animal that hunts other animals for food.

Prey: An animal that is hunted by other animals.

Pup: Baby dog, wolf, or other canid.

Radio transmitter: A radio antenna that sends out radio waves. Scientists track wolves' movements by fitting them with collars equipped with radio transmitters.

Scavenger: An animal that feeds on dead rather than live animals. Wolves are scavengers and will steal a meal stored by other predators.

Scent markings: The trail that wolves and other animals leave to mark their territory. Wolves have scent glands near their tails; they rub these glands on rocks and trees to leave a scent for other wolves to find.

Species: A group of animals that mate and produce offspring with each other but do not breed with other animals; an animal belonging to a biological classification.

Streamlined: Having a flowing shape that reduces resistance to water or air.

Submissive: A wolf that obeys another wolf's authority; also called a subordinate.

Territory: An area of land, including an animal's nesting or denning site, occupied and defended by an animal or group of animals.